Editor
Emily R. Smith, M.A. Ed.

Managing Editor
Karen J. Goldfluss, M.S. Ed.

Editor-in-Chief
Sharon Coan, M.S. Ed.

Illustrator
Ken Tunell

Cover Artist
Brenda DiAntonis

Art Coordinator
Kevin Barnes

Art Director
CJae Froshay

Imaging
Ralph Olmedo
Rosa C. See

Product Manager
Phil Garcia

Publisher
Mary D. Smith, M.S. Ed.

Spotlight
Lewis & Clark Expedition
and
The Louisiana Purchase

Author

Robert W. Smith

Teacher Created Resources, Inc.
6421 Industry Way
Westminster, CA 92683
www.teachercreated.com

ISBN: 978-0-7439-3233-2

©2003 Teacher Created Resources, Inc.
Reprinted, 2012
Made in U.S.A.

Teacher Created Resources

Table of Contents

Introduction 3

Teacher Lesson Plans
Reading Comprehension—The Louisiana Purchase 4
Reading Comprehension—The Lewis & Clark Expedition 4

Student Reading Pages
The Louisiana Purchase 5
Lewis & Clark Expedition 9

Reading Comprehension Quizzes
The Louisiana Purchase Quiz 15
The Lewis & Clark Expedition Quiz 16
The Members of the Corps of Discovery Quiz 17

Teacher Lesson Plans
Understanding and Using Maps 18
Written Language and Oral Discussion 18

Student Activity Pages
The Journey of Lewis & Clark 19
The Louisiana Purchase 20
The Growth of the United States 21
Native Americans on the Map 22
Journal Writing 23
Letters Home 24
Cultural Differences 25
Cultures on the Move 26

Teacher Lesson Plans
Nature Observations 27
Classroom Drama with Reader's Theater 27

Student Activity Pages
Keeping a Science and Discovery Journal 28
Studying Leaves 29
Flower Power 30
Reader's Theater Notes 31
Reader's Theater Script 32

Teacher Lesson Plans
Working with Time Lines 34
Famous People Research 34

Student Activity Pages
Time Line 35
Famous People of the 1700s and 1800s 36
Becoming a Famous Person Guidelines 37

Teacher Lesson Plans
Culminating Activity—Western History Day 40

Student Activity Pages
Building Models 42
Selected Literature Information 43

Glossary of Terms 44

Annotated Bibliography 45

Answer Key 47

Introduction

The *Spotlight on America* series is designed to introduce some of the seminal events in American history to students in the fourth through eighth grades. Reading in the content area is enriched with a balanced variety of activities in written language, social studies, oral expression, art, and science. The series is designed to make history literally come alive in your classroom and take root in the minds of your students. The reading selections and comprehension questions serve to introduce the Louisiana Purchase and the Lewis & Clark Expedition. They set the stage for activities in other subject areas.

Meriwether Lewis (ArtToday)

The Louisiana Purchase was the largest land deal in American history involving 828,000 square miles (2,140,000 square km) of territory in all or part of 15 states. The decision was both providential because the nation clearly wanted to expand into this fertile territory and controversial because of the constitutional and legal questions involved. (President Jefferson admitted he stretched the Constitution to the tearing point.)

The Lewis & Clark expedition may have been the most important journey of exploration in American history. In less than three years, the Corps of Discovery traveled over 8,000 miles (12,900 km) in territory that had never been explored and mapped. Inhabited by more than 40 Native American tribal groups who primarily knew only their local territories, the trans-Mississippi West was literally a blank spot of unknown land on the map. The men and one woman of the Corps walked, paddled, and rode across this wilderness teeming with unknown plants and animals and rife with danger and adventure.

The writing and discussion activities in this book are designed to help students sense the spirit and nature of these adventures. The research activities are designed to bring students literally into the buckskins and broadcloth of people as diverse as Meriwether Lewis, Napoleon Bonaparte, William Clark, York, Sacagawea, and John Colter. The culminating activities aim to acquaint students with the daily pursuits of Native Americans and these frontier explorers.

William Clark (ArtToday)

The science activities focus especially on the identification of new plants and animals in one of the most important science expeditions in American history. The trip also vastly increased cultural knowledge of Native Americans as well as information about geographical features and weather.

Enjoy using this book with your students and look for other books in this series.

Teacher Lesson Plans

Reading Comprehension—The Louisiana Purchase

Objective—Students will demonstrate fluency and comprehension in reading historically based text.

Materials—copies of *The Louisiana Purchase* (pages 5–8); copies of reading comprehension quiz entitled *The Louisiana Purchase Quiz* (page 15); additional reading selections from books, encyclopedia, and Internet sources for enrichment

Procedure

1. Reproduce and distribute *The Louisiana Purchase* (pages 5–8). Review pre-reading skills by briefly reviewing text and encouraging students to underline as they read, make marginal notes and list questions, and highlight unfamiliar words.
2. Assign the reading as classwork or homework. Allow adequate time for students to finish.
3. Talk about these discussion questions or others of your choosing with the students.
   - Why would the United States want the Louisiana territory?
   - Should a president break the law or "bend" the Constitution to accomplish his goals?
   - What might have happened if France had not sold the Louisiana territory to the United States?

Assessment—Have students complete the reading comprehension quiz entitled *The Louisiana Purchase* (page 15). Correct and evaluate the quiz for student understanding.

Reading Comprehension—The Lewis & Clark Expedition

Objective—Students will demonstrate fluency and comprehension in reading historically based text.

Materials—copies of the *Lewis & Clark Expedition* (pages 9–14); copies of reading comprehension quizzes entitled *The Lewis & Clark Expedition Quiz* and *The Members of the Corps of Discovery Quiz* (pages 16–17); additional reading selections from books, encyclopedia, and Internet sources for enrichment

Procedure

1. Reproduce and distribute the *Lewis & Clark Expedition* (pages 9–14). Review pre-reading skills by briefly reviewing text and encouraging students to underline as they read, make marginal notes and questions, and highlight unfamiliar words.
2. Assign the reading as classwork or homework. Allow adequate time for students to finish.
3. Talk about these discussion questions or others of your choosing with the students.
   - What were the major results of the expedition?
   - What would have happened if the expedition had failed?
   - What are some of the cultural differences and misunderstandings which occurred on the trip?

Assessment—Have students complete the reading comprehension quizzes entitled *The Lewis & Clark Expedition Quiz* and *The Members of the Corps of Discovery Quiz* (pages 16–17). Correct and evaluate the quizzes for student understanding.

The Louisiana Purchase

▶ The Land

The Louisiana territory extended from the Mississippi River to the Rocky Mountains and from the Gulf of Mexico to the Canadian border. It was an area of roughly 828,000 square miles (2,140,000 square km). The territory known as the Louisiana Purchase had been owned or claimed by France based on the explorations of men like René Robert Cavelier and Sieur de La Salle until 1763 when France gave these claims to Spain.

American citizens and leaders were especially interested in this land for two reasons. First, the western boundary of the United States at that time was the Mississippi River and some Americans already wanted to expand into the lands west of the Mississippi.

Secondly, western frontiersmen shipped farm goods for sale down the Mississippi River to New Orleans where they were exported to European markets without being taxed. These products included flour, whiskey, pork, salt, animal skins, tobacco, and cheese, among other goods. Permission to do this was known as the "right of deposit" which was negotiated between the United States and Spain in 1795. In 1798, Spain rescinded this right and made western farmers angry.

New Orleans, at the mouth of the Mississippi River on the Gulf of Mexico, was the only accessible port for western farmers. It was also the main administrative center for Spanish control of their territory. Much of the rest of the territory was largely unexplored and unknown.

▶ France Regains Control of Louisiana

In 1800, France, under the rule of Emperor Napoleon Bonaparte, negotiated a secret treaty with Spain and again took control of this territory. Spain retained its control of the area known as Spanish Florida, a narrow strip of land running from the Mississippi River to the Atlantic Ocean and including the Florida Peninsula. Bonaparte assigned an army to occupy the Louisiana territory, although Spanish authorities continued to govern the area. Spain even briefly allowed the "right of deposit" again.

▶ President Jefferson Tries to Acquire Louisiana

When Thomas Jefferson became the United States president in 1801, American representatives in Great Britain heard rumors that France was intending to rebuild its power and influence in North America. Jefferson and many other influential Americans were worried that a powerful European nation like France would interfere with the trade of its western settlers and with western expansion.

Jefferson told Robert Livingston, the new minister of the United States to France, to warn France that the United States was opposed to any transfer of Spanish colonies to any country other than the United States.

▶ Troubles for Napoleon

The French troops that Napoleon intended to send to occupy New Orleans and enforce French authority got diverted to Hispaniola, where the French had a colony. At the time, a rebellion against French rule was being led by the brilliant slave leader, Toussaint L'Ouverture. Although the French army put down the rebellion, they were severely weakened by diseases such as yellow fever and continuing battles with the rebels. They never got to New Orleans.

The Louisiana Purchase *(cont.)*

▶ Troubles for Napoleon *(cont.)*

Jefferson had Pierre du Pont de Nemours carry messages to Livingston and help him negotiate with the French government. The United States threatened to form an alliance with England against France if France took over Louisiana. Jefferson did this despite his strong pro-French and anti-British attitude during the American Revolution and the French Revolution of the 1790s.

▶ The Great Powers: Great Britain and France

The two great world powers of the time were Great Britain and France. Britain had a powerful navy, many colonies, a strong army, and wealth based on trade around the world. France had a very powerful and experienced army and was the strongest power in Europe. However, France had overthrown its monarchy, gone through a revolution, and was now led by a self-appointed dictator. Spain, a weaker country, was often allied with France.

On the other hand, the Unites States was struggling financially and had a very weak standing army and a small navy. The only advantage the United States had was that it bordered the territory in question.

Du Pont suggested offering to buy the Florida territory from Spain and feared that threats would make Napoleon even more stubborn about keeping the Louisiana territory. When the Spanish governor suspended the "right of deposit" again in 1802, western frontiersmen were ready to go to war. Secretary of State James Madison warned both Spain and France of possible war.

▶ Negotiating the Purchase

Jefferson sent James Monroe to join Livingston in efforts to buy the east bank of the Mississippi River, which would allow Americans access to the Gulf of Mexico. Congress had authorized two million dollars for this purpose. Jefferson suggested to the negotiators that they offer as much as nine million dollars for New Orleans and the Florida territory.

Napoleon was still interested in establishing a vast French empire in America to go along with his powerful European empire and strong French influence in other parts of the world. He even sent 15,000 more troops to Hispaniola. Nonetheless, another European war between Great Britain and France was clearly coming soon.

The American envoy warned Napoleon that the United States might form an alliance with Great Britain. The British navy could easily capture New Orleans and the American government was considering sending an army of 50,000 men to help in the capture of New Orleans.

Napoleon realized that holding the territory against an expanding United States might be both difficult and expensive. He was also aware that he needed funds to finance his upcoming war with England. Furthermore, he was not anxious to have the United States and Great Britain allied against him. His decision was opposed by both of his brothers whose advice he sometimes ignored and sometimes followed. He offered to sell the entire territory to the United States for 15 million dollars.

The Louisiana Purchase *(cont.)*

▶ Completing the Deal

The American negotiators, who knew they were exceeding their instructions, realized this was the deal of a century and accepted the offer. Jefferson knew the Constitution did not specifically authorize land purchases but it did permit treaties so he felt he could get it accepted in Congress.

Most congressmen knew this was a great deal even if they claimed to be upset over the way it was handled by the president. After a good deal of criticism in both houses of Congress over Jefferson's stretching of constitutional authority, they approved the treaty and agreed to spend the money. The government was so short of funds that they needed to borrow the money from European banks on 15-year loans.

The United States officially took possession of the Louisiana territory on December 20, 1803. Eventually, a few boundary adjustments were agreed upon and the United States acquired Spain's Florida territory as well in 1819.

▶ The Legacies

United States Doubles in Size

The consequences of the Louisiana Purchase were profound. In one single act, the Unites States doubled in size. A country that had been contained between the Atlantic Ocean and the Mississippi River now extended to the Rocky Mountains.

A Land Rich in Natural Resources

While much of the land had originally been considered a "great American desert," the explorations of Meriwether Lewis and William Clark clearly proved this was a rich and abundant land. Fifteen states were formed entirely or partly from this purchase. These include states such as Iowa, Kansas, and Nebraska, which form a large part of the "bread basket" of America. In these areas, rich soil produces important crops.

Access to the port of New Orleans gave western farmers an opportunity to export their products without being taxed by a foreign government. For much of the 19th century, the Mississippi River and its tributaries were the major routes for western commerce and travel.

Manifest Destiny

The purchase also strengthened American claims to the Oregon territory, which was previously claimed by several nations including Great Britain. This eventually put pressure on the British in the same way that the French were pressured to sell Louisiana. The Americans were physically close and a clear threat to settle the Oregon region. Britain had its Canadian colony but England was far removed from the action and keeping an army there would be expensive.

Spain felt the same pressure on its land in Florida and the Southwest. Eventually, these lands would also become part of the United States. Americans came to believe that they had a "Manifest Destiny" to extend from the Atlantic Coast to the Pacific Coast.

The Louisiana Purchase *(cont.)*

▶ The Principle People Involved

Thomas Jefferson

Thomas Jefferson was the main author of the Declaration of Independence. He served as a governor of Virginia and as a legislator. He was ambassador to France for the government of the United States after the American Revolution. George Washington appointed Jefferson as his first secretary of state, a job that carried the responsibility of dealing with foreign nations. In 1796, Jefferson was elected vice president of the United States and in 1800, he became the third president.

Jefferson was interested in acquiring control of the western half of North America. He had even paid a man to walk east from Sweden across Siberia through North America. (The man was stopped in Russia.) As president, Jefferson was determined to explore this territory and began to plan an expedition well before any hope existed of the land being purchased from France. Jefferson was a brilliant scientist, inventor, and architect. He developed new farming techniques, experimented with new plants, became a successful landscape designer, and was a self-taught violinist. Jefferson died on July 4, 1826, on the 50th anniversary of the proclamation of the Declaration of Independence.

Napoleon Bonaparte

Napoleon Bonaparte was born on the French-controlled island of Corsica. He was trained as an artillery commander in a French military academy. He quickly rose to power by demonstrating great military skill against France's European enemies and by recognizing whom to support in the shifting power struggles during the French Revolution. Napoleon used his popularity with soldiers to seize control of the French government in 1799. He intended to defeat France's enemies, especially England and Austria, and to increase France's power around the world.

Although he wanted to control a French empire in North America, he realized the Louisiana territory was vulnerable to attack. He also needed the money for a looming war with England. Napoleon spent much of his 16 years in power at war with various nations. He was finally defeated at Waterloo, one of the most famous battles in history, and exiled to the island of St. Helena where he died in 1821.

Robert Livingston

Robert Livingston was a New York representative to the Continental Congress. He helped Jefferson draft the Declaration of Independence. He served as a New York legislator, a judge, and a minister of foreign affairs for the United States government. He was minister of affairs to France where he was very instrumental in convincing the French to sell the Louisiana territory to the United States.

Other Influential People

James Monroe helped negotiate the Louisiana Purchase. There was some friction between Livingston and Monroe. Livingston felt he had done the groundwork for the purchase and Monroe was suspicious of being excluded from the negotiations. Samuel du Pont de Nemours was a French economist who had immigrated to the United States. Charles de Talleyrand was the French minister of foreign affairs. Toussaint L'Ouverture led a slave rebellion against French authority in Haiti.

Lewis & Clark Expedition

The Lewis & Clark Expedition is considered by some as the most important journey of exploration in American history. In less than three years, the members of the expedition traveled over 8,000 miles (12,900 km) by keelboat, canoe, horseback, and on foot across the American West from St. Louis, Missouri, to the Pacific Ocean and back.

President Thomas Jefferson instructed Lewis and Clark to accomplish five main goals on their expedition: to find the source of the Missouri River, to cross the Rocky Mountains, to follow the largest river west to the Pacific Ocean, to establish trade with the native peoples, and to assure the Native Americans of the peaceful intentions of the United States. To a remarkable extent, they accomplished these goals, despite the fact that no river existed to provide a direct water route to the Pacific Ocean.

▶ Starting Out—Up the Missouri

The men were trained by William Clark at Camp Wood where the Missouri River and Mississippi River converge. Clark was a tough but able instructor. During this time, Meriwether Lewis stayed in St. Louis making final arrangements and purchases for the journey. The 45-person expedition departed up the Missouri River on May 14, 1804.

They traveled on a flat-bottomed, raft-like keelboat and two large wooden dugout canoes called *pirogues.* Their supplies included fishing hooks, tools, medals with Jefferson's picture engraved on them, compasses and other scientific instruments, medicine, rifles, beads, knives, trading goods, and some food. The men had to row, sail, pole, and haul the keelboat with ropes against the rushing water caused by spring floods. They endured hail and soaking rains, mosquitoes, gnats, ticks, and illnesses. At night they stopped along the shore or on an island for safety.

En route they met members of several tribes including the Yankton Sioux who were friendly and helpful and the Teton (or Lakota) Sioux who knew they were coming and were not as friendly. The Teton Sioux were accustomed to charging fares for permission to cross their territory and the expedition was nearly destroyed here. Only the determination and quick wits of the leaders and some disagreement among the Sioux chieftains got them safely past.

During the 1,600-mile (2,570-km) trip up the Missouri River to its headwaters, they met members of other tribes, including the Arikaras who were at war with the Mandan Indians. Lewis and Clark had hoped to receive help from the Mandans and managed to arrange an uneasy peace between the warring tribes.

▶ Winter at Fort Mandan

Near the Mandan villages, the men built a series of eight connected log cabins in a V-shape with a fence over the open end. These buildings were called Fort Mandan. During their winter stay at Fort Mandan, Lewis and Clark caught up on their journals, directed the construction of six dugout canoes, talked to Native Americans and French fur trappers about the land to the west, and hired Toussaint Charbonneau and his Shoshone wife, Sacagawea, as guides and interpreters.

Lewis & Clark Expedition (cont.)

▶ Winter at Fort Mandan (cont.)

On April 7, 1805, the expedition sent several men back to St. Louis on a keelboat with over 100 plant samples, four magpies, one prairie dog, many animal skins and bones, bison robes, soil samples, Clark's maps, and a 45,000-word report from Lewis detailing everything they had learned about Native Americans, plants, animals, and even a total eclipse of the moon. All of this was to be delivered to President Jefferson.

▶ Heading into the Unknown

On the same day, 33 people left Fort Mandan heading west into unknown land. This Corps of Discovery included the two co-captains, 26 army volunteers, two French-Canadian interpreters, Sacagawea, her newborn baby (Jean Baptiste, born on February 11, 1805), Clark's personal slave named York, as well as Seaman, Lewis' large Newfoundland dog. They traveled in two large pirogues and the six dugout canoes they had made over the winter.

They headed west along the Missouri River to a point where it merges with the Marias River. They were uncertain of which fork of the river to follow. Although the rest of the expedition's members favored the northern fork, the leaders decided on the southern fork. After several days, Lewis, traveling ahead of the main party, found the Great Falls of the Missouri and knew they had come the right way. He also got chased by a grizzly bear, threatened by a mountain lion, and attacked by three bull bison in one afternoon.

They had to carry their supplies and canoes about 18 miles (29 km) around the Great Falls and several smaller falls. On May 26, 1805, Lewis was the first to see the Rocky Mountains. He realized then that no river existed to carry them over the mountains to the Pacific Ocean and that they would have to travel across the mountains with horses. They had to find the Shoshone tribe to ask for help.

▶ Finding the Shoshone

As they entered the territory of the Shoshone, Sacagawea recognized many landmarks. When she was 12 years old, she had been captured by the Hidatsa Indians and sold as a slave to her husband. When they reached the point at which the Missouri River splits into three branches, the captains named the rivers after important American leaders: Madison, Jefferson, and Gallatin. The expedition followed the newly named Jefferson River into Shoshone territory.

When Lewis and a few hunters finally met the Shoshones, the Native Americans thought the white explorers might be enemies or a trick arranged by the foes, the Blackfeet tribe. Sacagawea's arrival with the main group convinced them otherwise and she was joyfully reunited with her brother, Cameahwait, who was now chief of the tribe.

Cameahwait reluctantly agreed to trade some horses for guns, knives, clothes, and other trading goods. They hired another Shoshone they named "Old Toby" to guide them through the Bitterroot Mountains. The expedition used the horses to travel across the mountains into Nez Perce territory. Game was very sparse here. Snowy weather made travel difficult. The men were reduced to living on "portable soup," an unpleasant dried concoction that Lewis had purchased in St. Louis for emergency use. They also ate a horse, a coyote, bear oil, and crayfish.

Lewis & Clark Expedition *(cont.)*

▶ Following the Columbia

The Nez Perce provided important information so that the expedition could find their way to the Columbia River. The Nez Perce also saved them from starvation. The men were able to trade for food, including camas roots and dried salmon. Many of the members of the group became sick from this diet, but they eventually recovered.

The expedition made dugout canoes and paddled down the Clearwater, Snake, and Columbia Rivers encountering rapids and many other dangers on the way to the Pacific Ocean. On November 14, 1805, Lewis saw the Pacific Ocean for the first time.

▶ Winter at Fort Clatsop

The members of the expedition voted to stay on the coast for the winter and return the following spring. They built a fort called Fort Clatsop and spent the winter getting ready for the return trip. They did hope to encounter a sailing ship owned by fur traders and return by that route but no ship ever stopped.

▶ Heading Home

The expedition began the return trip on March 23, 1806. They went back up the Columbia River, which was much harder to travel on going against the current. They met Native American tribes they had encountered earlier and recovered their horses for the trip over the mountains. After a stormy trip through the mountains, they split the expedition into two groups.

Lewis led one group north on a route along the Marias River. Along the way, they had an encounter with unfriendly Blackfeet Indians. Lewis and his men had to ride 120 miles (193 km) in one day to escape the threat. Later, Lewis was shot in the upper leg by one of his men who had poor eyesight and mistook him for an elk.

Clark and his group went south and explored the Yellowstone River. Clark had half of his horses stolen by Crow Indians. His men built canoes and followed the Yellowstone River. Clark's group may have been one of the first expedition groups to see the land that is now Yellowstone National Park.

The two groups met at the junction of the Missouri River and the Yellowstone River on August 12, 1806. From there, they traveled together down the Missouri River.

▶ Home at Last

They reached Fort Mandan on August 17, 1806, and started down the Missouri River en route to St. Louis. They met the Teton Sioux again but passed through the area with less friction this time. They arrived in St. Louis on September 23, 1806. The entire journey had taken two years, four months, and nine days.

Most Americans had given them up for dead, although President Jefferson had not lost faith. Along the way, they discovered 178 new kinds of plants, 122 new species of animals, and more than 40 Native American tribes. Their expedition also helped establish the United States claim to the Oregon territory. The information they acquired about natural resources and Native American cultures was vitally important to the nation.

Lewis & Clark Expedition (cont.)

▶ The Members of the Corps of Discovery

Meriwether Lewis

Meriwether Lewis was born in Virginia in 1774. When his father died, his mother remarried and moved to Kentucky. Lewis inherited a plantation from his birth father and returned to Virginia as a young man to manage the plantation. He joined the Virginia militia in 1794 to help President Washington put down the Whiskey Rebellion, a farmer's revolt against federal taxes. Lewis transferred to the regular army and was assigned to a rifle company commanded by William Clark who became a close friend. He remained in the army, attaining the rank of captain in 1800.

In 1801, his Virginia neighbor, President Thomas Jefferson, chose Lewis to be his private secretary. Jefferson admired Lewis' character and intelligence. Jefferson was already planning a secret expedition into the territory held by Spain and France so he had Lewis trained in the classification and identification of plants as well as in natural history. In 1803, as the Louisiana Purchase was being completed, Jefferson sent Lewis to Philadelphia to learn botany, celestial navigation, and practical medicine.

Lewis chose Clark to be his co-leader because he thought that an expedition of this nature needed two men. They complemented each other and their personal friendship was so strong that they never had a serious disagreement on the entire trip.

After their return, Jefferson named Lewis governor of the Louisiana Territory, a job not as well fitted to his talents and personality. In 1809, Lewis died at the age of 35 on a trip to Washington. He had severely tangled finances, a drinking problem, some serious illnesses, and difficulties with some of his former associates. He either committed suicide or was murdered along a particularly dangerous trail called the Natchez Trace.

William Clark

William Clark was the ninth of ten children. His five brothers had all fought in the Revolutionary War and one of his brothers, General George Rogers Clark, was a national hero. His family was originally from Virginia but moved to the Kentucky wilderness where Clark became a skilled woodsman. Clark joined the local militia when he was 19 and had several encounters with Native Americans. He learned how to fight and negotiate with Native Americans without developing a hatred for them. In the army, he learned to construct forts, draw maps, and earn the respect of men.

He left the army in 1796 and inherited a family plantation from his father in 1799. He also inherited several slaves including York, who would accompany him on the journey. Clark and Lewis kept in touch and in 1803, Lewis offered him the job of co-captain. Clark was happy to accept.

Clark was not as skilled in the sciences as Lewis was, but he kept superb maps of the journey, had exceptional talent in wilderness travel, commanded men effectively, possessed excellent engineering skills for building forts and boats, and understood Native American temperaments very well.

Lewis & Clark Expedition *(cont.)*

▶ The Members of the Corps of Discovery *(cont.)*

William Clark *(cont.)*

After the journey, Clark became Superintendent of Indian Affairs and later a territorial governor. He was known as Red Hair Chief to many Native American tribes and negotiated more than 30 treaties with them. He was regarded as fair and honest in his dealings with all men.

Clark and Lewis remained lifelong friends and Clark helped settle Lewis' affairs after his death. In 1808, Clark married Julia Hancock, a girl he had met just before the expedition began and for whom he named a river. They had five children before her death. Clark later married Julia's cousin and outlived her too. He was a loving father, caring not only for his own seven children but for Sacagawea's two children as well. He died in 1838 at the age of 68 as one of the most admired men in the nation.

Toussaint Charbonneau

Toussaint Charbonneau, a French fur trapper, lived with the Hidatsa Indians. Lewis and Clark hired him as an interpreter. He had two wives, one of whom was Sacagawea. He left the other wife at the Mandan village when he departed on the expedition. Charbonneau spoke the Hidatsa language and French. He was often difficult and not always cool in an emergency.

Sacagawea

Sacagawea was captured by Hidatsa Indians when she was about 12 years old. Native American tribes often raided other tribes for captives. She lived with this tribe until she was sold to Charbonneau as his wife. She was invaluable in dealing with the Shoshone Indians. At one time along the trip, her boat was overturned and the cradle she used to carry her baby was washed away. However, she was able to save the captains' journals and other important equipment from being carried away.

Jean-Baptiste

Jean-Baptiste was the child born to Sacagawea on February 11, 1805. He was carried in a cradle on Sacagawea's back for the journey. He was nicknamed "Pomp" by Clark. Sacagawea asked Clark to raise the boy when he was older. At that time, he was brought to Clark in St. Louis to be cared for.

York

A slave inherited by Clark, York was a very important member of the team. He was extremely strong, skilled in hunting, and fascinating to many of the Native American tribes. The Arikaras had never seen a black man nor a man as large as York. One Native American even thought he was a white man who had been colored black, and he tried to rub off some of the color. His "buffalo hair" was another feature they considered special.

York enjoyed chasing the children and acting rather wild to impress the Native Americans. He was treated well and highly respected by other members of the expedition. York sought his freedom after the expedition returned home. Clark, in a rare act of unfairness, refused to free him. Finally, in 1811, Clark reluctantly gave York his freedom.

Lewis & Clark Expedition (cont.)

▶ The Members of the Corps of Discovery (cont.)

George Drouillard

Drouillard was a critical member of the team. He was the ablest hunter in the group and a superior marksman. He spoke French and several Native American languages. His mother was a Shawnee Indian and he understood and got along well with most Native Americans. He was very cool in a crisis.

Seaman

Lewis' black Newfoundland dog was always a matter of interest to the Native Americans who used dogs to guard camps, pull travois (a carrying pack for teepees and personal items), and as meat. On one occasion, Chinook Indians stole Seaman and Lewis sent three armed men with orders to shoot if the pet was not returned. On another occasion, Seaman was bitten by a beaver and nearly bled to death.

▶ Unusual Facts About the Expedition

- Only one member of the expedition died on the journey. Sergeant Charles Floyd died of a burst appendix. Although Lewis demonstrated real talent in medicine during the journey, no doctor could have helped Floyd because no successful treatment for appendicitis existed at that time.

- Lewis and Clark took turns leading the expedition, usually alternating every other day. They were remarkably open to shared leadership. The group was usually consulted on important decisions, although the captains didn't always follow the group's advice.

- Every member of the expedition had an equal vote in the decision to winter on the Pacific Coast or return immediately. This included Sacagawea and York. This could be considered the first important vote cast by a black slave or a Native American woman in United States history.

- Privates on the expedition were paid $5 a month. Sergeants made $8 a month. The sergeants and a few privates kept journals, as did the two captains.

- Lewis purchased an air gun for the trip. This gun could kill small game without sound. This gun and the cannon on the keelboat were impressive to the Native Americans.

- Among the animals that were discovered by the explorers, which had never been classified by scientists, were antelope, prairie dogs, white pelicans, jackrabbits, and coyotes.

- Jefferson considered botany the most important of all of the sciences because plants were the basic staples of life for men and animals.

- Jefferson and Lewis had created a secret code so that they could communicate privately. They never got to use the cipher code because the distances were too great.

- Lewis recorded and discovered 177 new plants. These included Osage orange (a tree favored by Native Americans for making bows), the prairie apple, Native American tobacco, camas (whose roots were used for food), and the sticky currant. Clark is credited with only one plant discovery.

- The Mandan tribe was virtually wiped out by smallpox, which they caught from white fur traders. They had no immunity to the disease and did not know to separate the sick to protect the others.

Name _____

The Louisiana Purchase Quiz

Directions: Read pages 5–8 about the Louisiana Purchase. Then, answer these questions based on the information in the selection. Circle the correct answer in each question below. Underline the sentence in the selection where the answer is found.

1. Who was president of the United States when the Louisiana Purchase was completed?
   a. James Monroe
   b. Thomas Jefferson
   c. George Washington
   d. James Madison

2. What did the "right of deposit" allow western farmers to do?
   a. settle New Orleans
   b. export goods from New Orleans
   c. settle in Louisiana
   d. trade with Native Americans

3. Who led a slave revolt in Hispaniola?
   a. Robert Livingston
   b. Napoleon Bonaparte
   c. Toussaint L'Ouverture
   d. Thomas Jefferson

4. How much money did Jefferson suggest that his negotiators offer for New Orleans and the Florida territory?
   a. 15 million dollars
   b. nothing
   c. 9 million dollars
   d. 2 million dollars

5. What effect did the purchase of Louisiana have on the United States?
   a. It immediately started a war.
   b. It doubled the country's size.
   c. It made the Native Americans rich.
   d. The country went bankrupt.

6. Which man was sent by the president and Congress to help Robert Livingston in the negotiations?
   a. Napoleon Bonaparte
   b. James Madison
   c. James Monroe
   d. Robert Cavelier

7. How many states were made entirely or partly from the Louisiana Purchase territory?
   a. 15
   b. 50
   c. 13
   d. 5

8. Who suggested to President Jefferson that the United States try to buy the Florida territory rather than threaten war?
   a. James Monroe
   b. Robert Livingston
   c. Spanish government
   d. Pierre du Pont

9. In what year was the Louisiana Purchase completed?
   a. 1819
   b. 1803
   c. 1801
   d. 1795

10. What was the approximate size of the Louisiana Purchase territory?
    a. 15,000,000 sq. miles (38,800,000 sq. km)
    b. 8,000,000 sq. miles (20,700,000 sq. km)
    c. 800,000 sq. miles (2,070,000 sq. km)
    d. 828,000 sq. miles (2,140,000 sq. km)

Name _____

The Lewis & Clark Expedition Quiz

Directions: Read pages 9–11 about the Lewis & Clark Expedition. Answer these questions based on the information in the selection. Circle the correct answer in each question below. Underline the sentence in the selection where the answer is found.

1. Which river was the first river Lewis and Clark traveled on as they began their journey?

   a. Jefferson River
   b. Missouri River
   c. Marias River
   d. Columbia River

2. The members of the expedition spent the first winter with which tribe of Native Americans?

   a. Mandan
   b. Teton Sioux
   c. Clatsop
   d. Shoshone

3. Lewis and Clark helped negotiate peace between the Mandans and which other tribe?

   a. Nez Perce
   b. Shoshone
   c. Arikaras
   d. Yankton Sioux

4. How many people were in the Corps of Discovery that left Fort Mandan for the West?

   a. 45
   b. 33
   c. 37
   d. 103

5. Cameahwait was the chief of what tribe?

   a. Sioux
   b. Shoshone
   c. Mandan
   d. Nez Perce

6. What did the captains need to buy from the Shoshone Indians?

   a. dugout canoes
   b. food
   c. guns
   d. horses

7. Where did the men live during their winter on the Pacific Coast?

   a. Fort Clatsop
   b. Fort Mandan
   c. Camp Wood
   d. Shoshone villages

8. Who shot Lewis in the leg?

   a. Blackfeet Indians
   b. William Clark
   c. one of his own men
   d. Shoshone Indians

9. How many kinds of plants did the expedition discover?

   a. 40
   b. 178
   c. 122
   d. several thousand

10. What is a *pirogue*?

   a. a keelboat
   b. a dugout canoe
   c. a rowboat
   d. a sailboat

Name _____

The Members of the Corps of Discovery Quiz

Directions: Read pages 12–14 about the Lewis & Clark Expedition. Answer these questions based on the information in the selection. Circle the correct answer in each question below. Underline the sentence in the selection where the answer is found.

1. Which member of the corps of discovery was a slave?

   a. William Clark   c. York
   b. George Drouillard   d. Toussaint Charbonneau

2. Who was captured by the Hidatsa Indians at the age of 12?

   a. Meriwether Lewis   c. Jean-Baptiste
   b. Sacagawea   d. Toussaint Charbonneau

3. Which interpreter was sometimes difficult to get along with and not always cool in an emergency?

   a. George Drouillard   c. Toussaint Charbonneau
   b. Sacagawea   d. William Clark

4. How did Charles Floyd die?

   a. shot by Native Americans   c. a burst appendix
   b. killed by a grizzly bear   d. trampled by a bison

5. What is botany?

   a. the study of plants   c. the study of the stars
   b. the study of animals   d. the study of Native Americans

6. Which tribe was almost wiped out by smallpox?

   a. Blackfeet   c. Mandan
   b. Teton Sioux   d. Hidatsa

7. Who was Jean-Baptiste Charbonneau?

   a. Sacagawea's son   c. a hunter
   b. an interpreter   d. a slave

8. Why did the Native Americans admire York?

   a. He was black.   c. He chased bison on foot.
   b. He was large and strong.   d. He played with children.

9. William Clark named a river in honor of which person?

   a. York   c. Julia Hancock
   b. Toussaint Charbonneau   d. his sister

10. Who was President Jefferson's private secretary before the expedition?

    a. Julia Hancock   c. William Clark
    b. Meriwether Lewis   d. Charles Floyd

Teacher Lesson Plans

Understanding and Using Maps

Objective—Students will learn to use and derive information from a variety of map forms.

Materials—copies of *The Journey of Lewis & Clark* (page 19); copies of *The Louisiana Purchase* (page 20); copies of *The Growth of the United States* (page 21); copies of *Native Americans on the Map* (page 22); copies of *The Lewis & Clark Expedition* (pages 9–14); atlases, almanacs, and other maps for reference and comparison

Procedure

1. Review the map shown on *The Journey of Lewis & Clark* (page 19). Point out some important features of the map to the students. Have the students review *The Lewis & Clark Expedition* (pages 9–14) reading assignment. Assign the map activity at the bottom of the page.

2. Review *The Louisiana Purchase* (page 20) and assign the activity that requires students to locate states formed by the Louisiana Purchase territory.

3. Review the map on *The Growth of the United States* (page 21) activity page. Have the students answer the questions on the bottom of the page.

4. Review the map on the *Native Americans on the Map* (page 22) activity page. Have the students answer the questions on the bottom of the page.

Assessment—Correct the activity pages with the students. Check for understanding and review the basic concepts.

* *

Written Language and Oral Discussion

Objective—Students will develop skills in expository writing using journal narratives, letters, and point-of-view essays.

Materials—copies of *Journal Writing* (page 23); copies of *Letters Home* (page 24); copies of *Cultural Differences* (page 25); copies of *Cultures on the Move* (page 26); books, encyclopedias, and Internet sources

Procedure

1. Review the format students should use for journal writing (date, first person, etc.). Distribute *Journal Writing* (page 23) and review the prompt with the students. Encourage the students to complete additional research on the topic.

2. Review the format for writing friendly letters. Distribute *Letters Home* (page 24) and review the letter-writing assignment.

3. Distribute *Cultural Differences* (page 25) and read over the quotation together. Have students complete the preparation work. Then pair the students and have them conduct the oral discussion assignment. Assign the point-of-view essay as homework.

4. Read and discuss *Cultures on the Move* (page 26). Assign the first-person essay about York and the letter or diary entry for Jefferson.

Assessment—Have students share stories, letters, and journals with the class.

Name _____

The Journey of Lewis & Clark

Directions: This map illustrates several important highlights of the Lewis & Clark Expedition. Study the map carefully. Match the correct number from the map to the event described below. Some numbers may be used more than once. Use the *Lewis & Clark Expedition* (pages 9–14) reading assignment to help you.

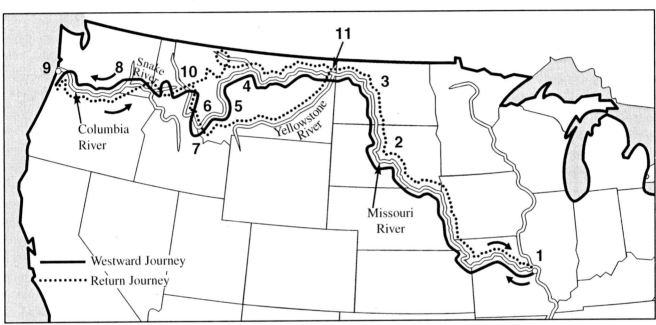

_____ The expedition started from here in 1804.

_____ The members of the expedition spent the winter of 1805 on the Pacific Coast.

_____ The captains made the decision to follow the south fork of the Missouri River.

_____ They built a fort and spent the winter preparing for the journey west.

_____ Lewis was threatened by a bear, a mountain lion, and three bull bison in one afternoon.

_____ The expedition had a serious and nearly deadly encounter with the Teton Sioux.

_____ The Snake and the Columbia Rivers meet here.

_____ The Missouri River splits into three branches. The captains named the rivers after important American leaders.

_____ They met the Shoshone and traded for horses.

_____ On the way east, the expedition split into two groups to explore different routes.

_____ Sacagawea and her husband are hired to be guides and interpreters.

_____ The expedition reunites for the return trip down the Missouri River.

_____ There are five waterfalls here on the Missouri River that the expedition had to walk around.

_____ The expedition ended here on September 23, 1806.

Name _____

The Louisiana Purchase

Directions: Study the map carefully. Use the map and other resources to answer the questions below.

1. In the chart below, list the 15 states that were partly or completely formed from the Louisiana Purchase.

2. Use an atlas, almanac, encyclopedia, or Internet resources to find the year each of these 15 states were admitted to the union. Add those dates to the chart below next to the appropriate states.

State	Date Admitted		State	Date Admitted

3. Use the Internet or other resources to identify the original states in the United States. List the states below.

_____   _____   _____

_____   _____   _____

_____   _____   _____

_____   _____   _____

_____

4. Research to find the four new states admitted to the union before the Louisiana Purchase. List them below.

_____   _____

_____   _____

Name _____

The Growth of the United States

Directions: Carefully study the map shown here and answer the questions on another sheet of paper. You may want to use the *Lewis & Clark Expedition* (pages 9–14) reading and *The Louisiana Purchase* (pages 5–8) reading to help you. You may also need to use other resources to locate these answers.

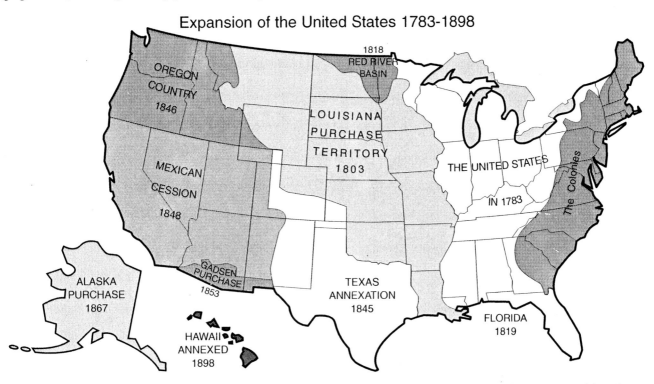

Expansion of the United States 1783-1898

1. Which land area did Thomas Jefferson and his ambassadors purchase when he was president?

2. Which area made up the United States during the Revolutionary War from 1776 to 1782?

3. What river formed the western border of the United States in 1800?

4. Which small area was acquired in 1818?

5. Describe the area that became part of the United States in 1819.

6. Which three territories came in the 1840s?

7. What piece of land was purchased in 1853?

8. Which came first: Texas, the Oregon country, or the land ceded (given up) by Mexico?

9. Alaska was the second largest purchase of land by the United States. In what year was it bought?

10. In what year did Hawaii become a part (a territory) of the United States?

11. Which two areas were explored by the Lewis & Clark expedition?

12. Which two states are not contiguous to (or touching) the rest of the United States?

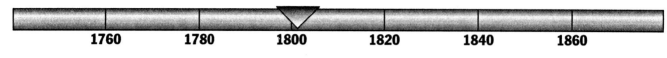

Name _____

Native Americans on the Map

Directions: Carefully study the map shown here and answer the questions on another sheet of paper. Use a resource map with the states labeled to help you.

1. List five tribes that belonged to the culture of the Plains Native Americans.

2. List three tribes that belonged to the culture of the California-Intermountain Native Americans.

3. Name two Pacific Coast tribes.

4. To which cultural group do the Hidatsa and the Mandan belong?

5. To which cultural group do the Flathead and the Nez Perce belong?

6. To which cultural group do the Shoshone and the Bannock belong?

7. To which cultural group do the Sioux and the Osage belong?

8. To which cultural group do the Blackfeet and the Crow belong?

9. In which state did the Mandan live?

10. In which state did the Nez Perce live?

11. In which state did the Kiowa live?

12. In which state did the Yakima live?

13. Name one state in which Blackfeet lived.

14. Were the Apache a member of the Plains Native American cultural group?

15. Name two tribes that lived near the Flathead tribe.

16. What state was named after the Kansa Indians?

Name _____

Journal Writing

In this journal entry, Lewis has examined the Great Falls of the Missouri and has just shot a bison when he encounters a more dangerous animal.

Friday June 14th 1805

". . . and having entirely forgotten to reload my rifle, a large white, or reather brown bear, had perceived and crept on me within 20 steps before I discovered him; in the first moment I drew up my gun to shoot, but at the same instant recolected that she was not loaded and that he was too near for me to hope to perform this opperation before he reached me, as he was then briskly advancing on me; . . . I had no sooner terned myself about but he pitched at me, open-mouthed and full speed, I ran about 80 yards and found he gained on me fast, I then run into the water . . . ."

Directions

1. Read at least one story or book about the Lewis & Clark Expedition.

2. Read over the *Lewis & Clark Expedition* (pages 9–14) again and review the maps you studied in the previous activity.

3. Use the Internet or other sources to review some journal entries from the expedition.

4. Review several Internet sites and interactive websites to get a feel for the many adventures that the members of the expedition encountered.

5. Write a response to the prompt below.

Writing Prompt

You have just traveled back in time to become a member of the Lewis & Clark Expedition. You may pretend to be a real member such as Meriwether Lewis, William Clark, York, John Colter, George Drouillard, Sacagawea, Toussaint Charbonneau, the baby Jean-Baptiste, or even Seaman, the dog. Or, you may just be yourself traveling as a member of the Corps of Discovery.

Using a journal format (where the entries note the day, month, and year and are written in the first-person format), describe what happened to you and other members of the expedition. Try to be as accurate as possible about names, places, events, animals you encounter, Native American tribes you meet, and how you travel at different stages of the journey. Don't forget to include battles, troubles on the rivers, dangerous animals, the weather, food shortages, insects, and all of the hardships of the journey.

Name _____

Letters Home

The men who started on the expedition weren't sure if they would make it back home or even that they would ever be heard from again.

Honored Parence.   **Camp River Dubois April the 8th 1804**

"*. . . I now embrace this oppertunity of writing to you once more to let you know where I am and where I am going. I am well thank God, and in high Spirits. I am now on an expidition to the westward, with Capt. Lewis and Capt. Clark, who are appointed by the President of the United States to go on an expidition through the interior parts of North America . . . I have Recd. no letters Since Betseys yet, but will write next winter if I have a chance. Yours, &c.*"

John Ordway Sergt.

Most Americans, including the men on the expedition, had received little or no schooling. Lewis had a few years at local schools, and Clark may have been taught the basics of reading and writing by his older brothers. Neither man had been to college. Spelling and grammar had not been standardized yet, so people often spelled words different ways. The word mosquitoes is spelled 15 different ways in journals of the expedition. Usage for periods, capitals, and commas varied as well.

Assignment

1. Write a letter to a friend. Assume your friend has never been to school in the United States and speaks only basic English. Describe what you do in school in each subject, at recess, and at lunch. Relate any interesting things that happen to you or your friends during the school day. In addition, tell how you spend the rest of the day after school—where you go, what you do, and how you spend the evening. Use the correct format for a friendly letter.

2. Then, write a letter from your friend back to you. Remember that this friend has never been to school in the United States. How might his or her letter be formatted differently than yours? Would the spelling be the same throughout? Would he or she use the friendly letter format that you have learned in your classroom? In the response letter, be creative about how this friend might write a letter back to you in English.

Name _____

Cultural Differences

> *The members of the expedition were constantly exposed to cultural differences among the Native American peoples. For example, they had learned to eat dog meat with one tribe and found other tribes that considered the practice degrading.*

Assignment

1. Use a variety of sources to research how members of the expedition got along with Native Americans. These sources could include books about the expedition, Internet sites about Lewis and Clark, textbooks, or encyclopedias.

2. Take notes on the interactions of the Native Americans and the expedition members. Try to find information related to each of these tribes.

Arikara	Mandan	Nez Perce
Hidatsa	Teton Sioux	Shoshone
Blackfeet	Clatsop	Crow
Chinook	Yakima	Yankton Sioux

3. Re-create this chart to organize your data for each Native American tribe.

Tribe Name	
Native American Reactions to the Visitors	
Attitudes Toward the Native Americans	
Problem for the Expedition	
How Problem was Solved	

4. Choose a partner to work with you if your teacher has not assigned one to you. One partner assumes the point of view of one Native American tribe. The other partner assumes the point of view of one of the members of the expedition. Conduct a discussion explaining the behavior and attitude of the point of view you have taken. Be as detailed and complete as possible. After you have practiced, you may be responsible for conducting your discussion in front of the class.

5. Use the information you acquired to write a three-paragraph essay defending your point of view either as a Native American or a member of the expedition. Use one paragraph to describe your behavior and attitudes. Use the second paragraph to describe how the other side behaved. Use the third paragraph to defend your point of view of the situation.

Name _____

Cultures on the Move

The Lewis & Clark Expedition involved many different cultures meeting and reacting with each other. Each Native American tribe had its own cultural heritage, beliefs, reactions to new things, and behaviors. There were also French fur trappers who lived with the Native Americans and often assumed some of the Native American cultures. The members of the expedition were usually English-speaking frontiersmen, many of whom had experience in frontier and Native American conflicts. York was unique. He was a black slave. Many Native Americans had never seen a black man and they were often fascinated with him.

10th of October Wednesday 1804

". . . Those Indians wer much astonished at my Servent, they never Saw a black man before, all flocked around him & examind him from top to toe, he Carried on the joke and made himself more turribal than we wished him to doe."—Clark

Assignment

1. Read as much as you can about Clark's slave named York.

2. Imagine that you are York and are traveling with the Lewis & Clark Expedition. In some kind of visual graphic organizer (web, cluster list, chart, etc.) describe how you would feel as a slave traveling with free white men and meeting Native Americans who lived in freedom on the plains. Tell how you would feel meeting tribes with strange and unusual customs. How do you feel as an object of attention by the Native Americans?

3. Then, write an essay describing your feelings and hopes. Write it in the first person format speaking as York.

4. Next, travel back in time before the Lewis & Clark Expedition. You have to imagine that you are President Thomas Jefferson. You desperately want to get access to the port at New Orleans and would like to expand the nation further to the west. Consider the fact that your country is very poor and the army is small and weak. You are worried about having a great power like France in the West. You also know that you do not have authority from Congress to negotiate a large land purchase. Write a letter or diary entry describing your efforts to solve your problems. Explain why this western territory is important. Describe your feelings and personal reactions when Napoleon agreed to sell the Louisiana Purchase.

Teacher Lesson Plans

Nature Observations

Objective—Students will maintain a journal of nature observations, learn to classify leaves according to specific criteria, learn the basic parts of a flower, and use evaporation to desalinate water.

Materials—copies of *Keeping a Science and Discovery Journal* (page 28); copies of *Studying Leaves* (page 29); copies of *Flower Power* (page 30); manila paper or construction paper; various leaves and flowers; salt; water; cups; plates

Procedure

1. Distribute and review *Keeping a Science and Discovery Journal* (page 28) with the students. Review the concept of a nature journal with the class using the assignment on this sheet. Determine the length of time you would like the students to keep their journals and assign the journals to the class. You will need to monitor progress on a daily or weekly basis in order to ensure that your students are keeping up with the assignment.

2. Review the leaf patterns on the *Studying Leaves* (page 29) activity sheet. After talking about the various patterns, assign the scrapbook and collection activity described at the bottom of the page.

3. Review the parts of a flower on the *Flower Power* (page 30) activity sheet. Assign the collection and pressed flowers activity. As an extension of this, review the process of desalinating water and complete the evaporation extension project described on the activity page.

Assessment—Determine a standard basis of comparison for the nature journals, leaf collections, and pressed flower scrapbooks.

Classroom Drama with Reader's Theater

Objective—Students will learn to use their voices effectively in dramatic reading.

Materials—copies of *Reader's Theater Notes* (page 31); copies of *Reader's Theater Script* (pages 32–33); various sources about the Louisiana Purchase and the Lewis & Clark expedition

Procedure

1. Review the basic concept of Reader's Theater with the class. The *Reader's Theater Notes* (page 31) page will help you to stress the important skills.

2. Have the students read over the *Reader's Theater Script* (pages 32–33). Place them into small groups and allow time to practice reading the script over several days.

3. Schedule class performances and have students share the prepared script.

4. Then, use the suggestions on the bottom of *Reader's Theater Notes* (page 31) to assign topics to teams of students. Allow student teams time to write and practice their own group scripts.

5. Schedule classroom performances of these scripts.

Assessment—Base performance assessments on pacing, volume, expression, and focus of the participants. Student-created scripts should demonstrate general writing skills, dramatic tension, and good plots.

Name _____

Keeping a Science and Discovery Journal

Sept. 7, 1804 (Approx. 25 miles above the Niobrara River)

"... discovered a Village of small animals that burrow in the grown ... Killed one and Caught one a live by poreing a great quantity of Water in his hole ... Those Animals are about the Size of a small Squirel Shorter (or longer) and thicker; the head much resembling a Squirel in every respect, except the ears which is Shorter, his tail like a ground squirrel which they shake & whistle when allarm'd. the toe nails long, they have fine fur and the longer hairs is gray ...."—Clark

July 1, 1806 (Vic. of Lolo, Montana)

"The little animal found in the plains of the Missouri which I have called the barking squirrel weighs from 3 to 3 1/2 pounds, it's form is that of a squirrel. it's colour is an uniform light brick red grey, the red reather predominating. the under side of the neck and belley are lighter coloured than the other parts of the body. The legs are short, and it is wide across the breast and sholders ... the head is also bony muscular and stout ... the upper lip is split or divided to the nose. the ears are short ...."—Lewis

Assignment

1. Use the descriptions from the two journal entries to write a paragraph describing the appearance and behavior of the prairie dog.

2. Find as many differences in usage and spelling as you can between the written language of Lewis and Clark and today's standard English.

3. Your next assignment is to begin keeping a nature journal for yourself. You need to include in this journal observations and sketches about the plants and animals you encounter. Your teacher will tell you for how long you must keep this journal.

4. Your descriptions should include colors, behaviors, estimated measurements, shapes, and comparisons to other plants and animals that you know.

5. You need to write at least one entry each day. Open fields, gardens, lawns, parks, and similar areas all have lots of plants, insects, lizards, and other wildlife for you to observe.

6. List the observations and draw sketches of either an entire item or just specific parts of the plant or animal.

7. Sketch and describe any animal tracks you see. You could also include descriptions of fur, feathers, shed skins, or other animal parts you discover.

Name _____

Studying Leaves

Parts of a Leaf

Meriwether Lewis was well trained in the study of plants. You can learn to describe leaves using a few basic terms. Many leaves have a midrib running down the center of the leave and veins branching off. The petiole supports the flat part of the leaf and is attached to the stem.

Vein Patterns

Most leaves are arranged in one of these vein patterns: palmate (shaped like the palm of a hand), pinnate (shaped like a feather), or parallel (veins go top to bottom).

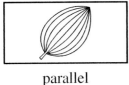
parallel   palmate
                                               pinnate

Edges

Many leaves have one of these patterns on the edges: smooth, serrated or toothed, or lobed.

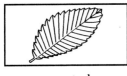      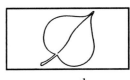
serrated   lobed   smooth

Leaf Arrangements

Leaves on a stem are often arranged in one of these patterns: opposite (right across from each other), alternate (first one leaf, then another), or whorled (several leaves at one point).

   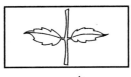   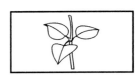
alternate   opposite   whorled

Assignment

1. Collect as many different kinds of leaves as you can from as many plants as you can. If possible, pick up leaves that have already fallen to the ground rather than pulling them from the trees.

2. Make a scrapbook using manila paper or construction paper.

3. Carefully attach one or two leaves to each page.

4. Label the vein pattern, edge pattern, and leaf arrangements for each leaf.

5. Describe the kind of plant from which each leaf came.

Name _____

Flower Power

Parts of a Flower

Lewis described many flowers in his journals. The flower is the part of a plant that allows it to produce seeds for reproduction. Study this picture with the parts of a flower labeled for you.

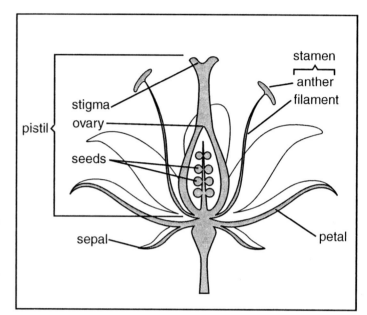

1. The petals attract insects for pollination.

2. The sepals support the petals.

3. The stamen is the male part of the flower. Pollen grains are produced in the anther.

4. The pistil is the female part of the flower. Pollen grains collect in the stigma. Seeds are produced in the ovary.

Assignment

1. Collect as many different types of flowers as you can. If possible, find flowers that have already been picked or have been broken off the plants rather than picking live flowers yourself.

2. Notice the plant from which each flower comes.

3. Carefully arrange several flowers on one sheet of white construction paper or manila paper.

4. Place another sheet of paper on top of the flowers.

5. Use a set of books or a heavy board to press the flowers down for a few days.

6. Uncover the flowers and neatly tape them to the bottom paper.

7. Connect several pages of pressed flowers with string or a metal clamp to make a flower scrapbook.

Extension Activity

At Fort Clatsop, the men boiled ocean water in order to desalinate it (to remove the salt). Humans and mammals need some salt in their diet, but ocean water has too much salt to be consumed. You can desalinate water in this manner. You need a hot or windy day. Mix two teaspoons of salt in a cup with four ounces of water. Stir the mixture until all of the salt is dissolved. Take the mixture outside and pour it into a plastic-coated paper plate, a metal pan, or a dinner plate. If the plate is light, place a rock in the plate or tape the plate down so that it doesn't blow over in the wind. Wait several hours until some or all of the water has evaporated. Examine the salt crystals that remain on the plate.

Name _____

Reader's Theater Notes

Reader's Theater is drama without costumes, props, stage, or memorization. It is done in the classroom by groups of students who become the cast of the dramatic reading.

Staging

Your classroom is the stage. Place four or five stools or chairs in a semicircle at the front of your class or in a separate staging area. You may use simple costumes, but generally no costumes are expected or used in this type of dramatization. If you have plain robes or simple coats of the same color or style so that everyone looks about the same, this can have a nice effect. Students dressed in the same school uniform or colors create an atmosphere of seriousness. Props are not needed, but they may be used for additional details.

Scripting

Each member of your group should have a clearly marked, useable script. You will have a chance to practice several times before presenting in front of the class.

Extensions

Feel free to add movement and memorization to performances. You can introduce mime to the performance and add props or costumes, as the circumstances allow. Some actors may even begin to add accents as they become more familiar with the format.

Assignment

1. Complete the *Reader's Theater Script* (pages 32–33) about the Lewis & Clark Expedition. Work within your group to prepare for the performance and share your interpretation of the script with the class.

2. Next, you get a chance to write and perform your own Reader's Theater script. Write a script based on one of the following events or another one related to the Louisiana Purchase or the Lewis & Clark Expedition.

   - Napoleon deciding to sell Louisiana to the United States
   - Jefferson and Lewis plan the expedition.
   - The expedition tries to decide which branch of the Missouri to follow.
   - Life at Fort Mandan with the Native Americans
   - The conflict with the Teton Sioux
   - Hard times crossing the mountains
   - Lewis and Clark report back to President Jefferson.

3. After practicing your script, share your performance with the rest of the class.

Reader's Theater Script

This script is an abbreviated account of the meeting between the expedition and the Shoshone people. (Much of the actual communication was done in sign language, the universal language of the Plains Native Americans, and with translations from English to French to Hidatsa to Shoshone and back.) This script requires the use of five speakers.

Homecoming

Narrator: The members of the Lewis & Clark Expedition have reached the headwaters of the Missouri River where it divides into three rivers. Following the Jefferson fork, the captains are desperate to find the Shoshone Indians in order to get horses and to find a route over the Rocky Mountains. They are now sure that no river exists to carry them over the mountains and they have to have horses for travel over the mountains. Captain Lewis and two men have gone on ahead to find the Shoshone and scout the trail.

Captain Lewis: George, we have to find the Shoshone soon. If it gets any closer to winter, we'll never make it over those mountains.

George Drouillard: The Shoshone woman said we are close. She was captured from her village near the three forks of the Missouri, which we just passed a few days ago. She remembered that mountain that looks like a beaver's head. We've got to be going in the right direction.

Lewis: There's a Native American up ahead. He must be Shoshone. Let's catch up with him.

Narrator: The men race after the Shoshone, but he vanishes. Soon they come upon three Shoshone women gathering roots for food.

Lewis: Please listen to me. We have come a long way to meet the Shoshone people. Please take these gifts and lead us to your village where we may talk with your chief.

Narrator: The two girls and the older women are terrified by the appearance of these explorers but they are gratified by the gifts. They agree to lead them to their camp. As Lewis approaches the camp with his men and the three women, he puts his rifle away as a sign of his peaceful intentions and takes out an American flag which he carries. A huge crowd of Shoshone suddenly surround them and escort them to the village where the three women display their gifts. The leader, Chief Cameahwait, approaches them. He is not too friendly or trusting.

Cameahwait: Who are you? Why have you come to our village?

Lewis: I represent the president of the United States in Washington. We are on a great journey to the far ocean beyond the mountains.

Reader's Theater Script *(cont.)*

Homecoming *(cont.)*

Cameahwait: I do not know or care about this president. Why do you come to our village? Who sent you?

Lewis: We have come to bring gifts to your people and to trade for horses which we need to go over the mountains. We also need to find the pass through these mountains.

Cameahwait: I think that you come as an enemy. I have heard of white people but I have never seen one. We have no horses to trade. I do not trust you. We should kill you now.

Lewis: I come with many people. They are carrying many gifts and many goods for trade. We travel with a Shoshone woman, who has a child. We come in peace. A war party does not travel with a woman or child. She has shown us the way to her homeland so that she can see her people again. She was captured four years ago by the Hidatsa Indians.

Cameahwait: Maybe the Blackfeet or the Hidatsa have sent you as a trick.

Lewis: We have nothing to hide. We travel with many things you have never seen before. Besides the Shoshone woman, we have a black man who wears buffalo hair. He is a giant among men. We have many guns and much ammunition and a gun which kills in silence.

Cameahwait: Where are these marvels? I think you are sent by the Blackfeet.

Narrator: A Shoshone scout reports that he has seen a great group of men, including one black man and a Native American woman carrying a child. As the group enters the camp, Sacagawea comes forward. Suddenly, she points to her mouth to indicate she is one of them. She looks very carefully at Cameahwait and then covers him with her robe or blanket to indicate they are related.

Sacagawea: My brother, Cameahwait! My brother, do you not remember your sister? Do you recognize the little sister who used to tease you all the time? Do you remember your sister?

Cameahwait: My sister, you have returned from the dead. Come, we must have a great feast to celebrate your return. Bring your friends into our village. Let me see the wonders you have brought.

Teacher Lesson Plans

Working with Time Lines

Objective—Students will learn to derive information from a time line and make time lines relevant to them.

Materials—copies of *Time Line* (page 35); copies of *The Louisiana Purchase* (pages 5–8); copies of *The Lewis & Clark Expedition* (pages 9–14); research resources including books, encyclopedias, texts, atlases, almanacs, and Internet sites

Procedure

1. Collect all available resources for your students so that they have plenty of places to find information.

2. Reproduce and distribute the *Time Line* (page 35) activity sheet. Review the concept of a time line, possibly using the school year as an example.

3. Review the various events listed on the time line activity sheet.

4. Assign students to find additional dates for the time line as described in the assignment at the bottom of the page.

5. Students may want to use the readings from previous lessons to locate additional dates for their time lines.

6. Have students create their own personal time lines as described in the assignment at the bottom of the page.

Assessment—Share additions to time line in classroom discussion using a board or chart to list the new dates. Have students share their personal time lines in small groups.

* *

Famous People Research

Objective—Students will develop skills in finding, organizing, and presenting research information.

Materials— copies of *Famous People of the 1700s and 1800s* (page 36); copies of *Becoming a Famous Person Guidelines* (pages 37–39); books, encyclopedias, and Internet sources

Procedure

1. Review list of potential famous people on the *Famous People* (page 36) sheet. Solicit other suggestions and add those to the sheet.

2. Review the information shared on the *Becoming a Famous Person Guidelines* (pages 37–39) sheets. Stress organizing material, studying notes, and techniques for presentations. Then, review the research guidelines.

3. Allow students time to prepare their research-based presentations. Then, arrange a schedule of presentations.

Assessment—Assess students on the basis of their written notes and oral presentations.

Name _____

Time Line

1770   William Clark is born in Virginia.

1774   Meriwether Lewis is born in Virginia.

1776   The Declaration of Independence is proclaimed.

1783   The Treaty of Paris ends the Revolutionary War.

1789   George Washington is inaugurated as president of the United States.

1795   Spain allows American settlers "right of deposit" for goods in New Orleans.

1797   John Adams becomes president of the United States. Thomas Jefferson is vice president.

1798   Spain suspends "right of deposit."

1800   Spain transfers Louisiana territory to France.

1801   Jefferson becomes the third president of the United States.

Lewis is appointed secretary to Jefferson.

"Right of deposit" is reinstated.

1802   "Right of deposit" is suspended again.

1803   British ships are blockading some French ports.

United States purchases Louisiana Territory from France.

Lewis and Clark are appointed to lead an expedition across the West.

1804   The expedition leaves from Camp Wood near St. Louis.

Aaron Burr kills Alexander Hamilton in a pistol duel.

1805   Sacagawea's baby is born just before the expedition leaves Fort Mandan.

1806   The expedition returns to St. Louis.

Zebulon Pike explores the southwestern United States and discovers Pike's Peak.

1807   Clark is named Superintendent of Indian Affairs for the Louisiana territory.

Lewis is appointed governor of the Louisiana territory.

1808   Clark marries Julia Hancock.

1809   Lewis dies on the Natchez Trace in Tennessee.

Jefferson leaves the White House after eight years as president.

1813   Clark becomes governor of the Louisiana territory.

1838   Clark dies in St. Louis.

Assignment

1. Study the time line above.

2. Find 10 dates for events in American history to add to the time line. They may go before, during, or after the time line. Make a list of these dates and be prepared to share them with the class. Be sure you know a little bit of background information about each of your additional dates.

3. Next, you need to create a time line of your own personal lifetime since the year you were born. Include some important events in your life. Then add events that happened in your country and the world during the same time. These events might include terrorist attacks, presidential elections, important people who died, as well as sporting events and other happenings in popular culture.

Famous People of the 1700s and 1800s

The Louisiana Purchase

Napoleon Bonaparte—leader of the most powerful army in Europe
Aaron Burr—schemer who tried to get control of the western United States
Thomas Jefferson—president of the United States
Robert Livingston—chief negotiator of the treaty
Toussaint L'Ouverture—black revolutionary leader in Haiti
James Monroe—special American ambassador; later president
Charles Talleyrand—tricky French minister of foreign affairs

Lewis & Clark Expedition

Toussaint Charbonneau—Sacagawea's husband and
    French interpreter
William Clark—co-captain of the expedition
John Colter—hunter; scout; later mountain man and explorer
Pierre Cruzatte—one-eyed master boatman; fiddle player
George Drouillard—hunter; interpreter; extremely valuable
Patrick Gass—sergeant; superior woodsman; kept journal
Meriwether Lewis—co-captain of the expedition
Sacagawea—Shoshone interpreter and guide
York—slave who fascinated Native Americans

Other Famous Explorers of the Period

James Beckwourth—African-American scout; fur trader
Daniel Boone—famous explorer who opened the Kentucky territory
James Bowie—adventurer and Texas hero
Davy Crockett—famous explorer; frontiersman; congressman
Hugh Glass—mountain man; adventurer
Jean Lafitte—pirate; hero in War of 1812
Zebulon Pike—explorer of the American Southwest
Jedediah Smith—explorer and adventurer

Other Famous People of the Period

John Jacob Astor—fur trade; wealthy American
Benjamin Banneker—African-American inventor; scientist
James Fenimore Cooper—popular novelist of the frontier
Dorothea Dix—reformer who helped the mentally ill
Deborah Sampson Gannett—first woman soldier
Sarah Josepha Hale—first female editor
Alexander Hamilton—war hero; important government leader
Andrew Jackson—war hero; first frontier president
Marquis de Lafayette—hero of American Revolution and French Revolution
James Madison—"Father of the Constitution"; later president
Sequoya—developed first written Native American language
Henry David Thoreau—writer and naturalist
George Washington—war leader; first United States president
Emma Willard—founded first female academy

Name _____

Becoming a Famous Person Guidelines

Select a Person

Choose a person from the suggested list or choose anyone from the late 1700s or early 1800s who had an impact on American history. Be certain that you choose someone who interests you and will hold your attention. Before you finalize your choice, make sure that you can find several books in the library and websites about your person.

Complete the Research

Use the research model on these pages to find out everything you can about the person. Know the important dates, the vital statistics, the personal life, and the struggles of your famous person. Become familiar with your person's accomplishments. Begin to think of yourself as that person. Try to assume the attitude and the personality of your person.

Go to the Sources

1. Use encyclopedias, almanacs, biographies, the Internet, and other sources of information to acquire the basic information you need.

2. You should find and use at least two full-length biographies about your person. You can also use adult biographies to research material not available in children's books. Use the index and table of contents of these higher-level books to locate some information you need to know more about.

Take Careful Notes

- Use your own words.
- Write your facts clearly and briefly.
- Write down the basic facts in an orderly way. (The outline on the next page shows one good format to use.)
- Look for anecdotes and funny stories about your person.
- Study the notes.
- Get a friend to quiz you about your person so that you know what you need to study and are confident about what you know.

Find a Costume and Props

1. Put together an appropriate costume. Check your closets at home for pants, slacks, shirts, or old costumes that might work. Check with parents, grandparents, older siblings, and friends for articles of clothing that might help. Ask for help getting to thrift stores for the missing pieces.

2. Don't wear tennis shoes. (They weren't invented yet.) Use or borrow moccasin-like bedroom slippers, leather boots, or leather shoes. If they're too big, stuff the toes with tissues before putting them on for your presentation.

3. Try to use a prop that fits with your character. A journal for Lewis or a compass for Clark are two examples of effective props.

Becoming a Famous Person Guidelines *(cont.)*

Be Your Famous Person

1. "My name is . . . . What would you like to know about me?" This is one way to begin your presentation. You might also want to give a brief presentation listing five or six important facts about yourself as this famous person. This will give your classmates a place to begin with their questions. Have a story to tell or something else to say if there is a momentary lull in the questioning.

2. Don't forget who you are and stay in character for your entire presentation. You are a famous person—not another student in the class. Be very serious. Avoid any silly behaviors.

3. At the end of the questions, review the important facts about your life.

Be Dramatic

- Use a loud voice. Don't drop your voice at the end of sentences.
- Use gestures. Use your arms and prop to emphasize your points.
- Be forceful, assertive, and self-assured.
- Have faith in yourself.

Assignment

Directions: Use this outline form to help you find and note important information about your famous person.

I. Youth
  A. Birth place and date
  B. Home life and experiences
    1. Siblings and parents
    2. Places lived (parts of the country; farm or town)
    3. Circumstances (rich or poor; important events)
    4. Age when you left home
  C. Schooling (when and how much)
  D. Interesting facts and stories about your youth

II. Adult Life
  A. Adventures and experiences
    1. Give details of each adventure or experience
    2. Fights and wars
    3. Friends and companions in your adventures
  B. Lifestyle and personal habits
    1. Personal attitude toward life (list examples)
    2. Were you a risk-taker or cautious? (give examples)
    3. Personal behavior (cruel, kind, honest, etc.)
    4. Leadership experiences (Did men follow you? Why?)
    5. Physical abilities and disabilities (illnesses; physical problems)

Becoming a Famous Person Guidelines *(cont.)*

Assignment *(cont.)*

II. Adult Life *(cont.)*
   C. Personal information
      1. Marriage/children
      2. Jobs held
      3. Adult hobbies and interests
   D. Reasons for fame
      1. Firsts (anything you accomplished first in human history)
      2. Inventions and discoveries (give complete details)
      3. Contributions to the human race or destructive acts (give details and reasons you did what you did)
      4. Greatest challenges you faced (describe and explain)
      5. Impact on United States or the world (importance of what you did)

III. End of Life
   A. Death
      1. Date of death
      2. Age when you died
      3. Cause of death (facts about the death)
      4. Other facts about your death
      5. Last words spoken (if known)
   B. Fame
      1. Were you famous at the time of death?
      2. Were you admired or forgotten by the time of your death?

IV. The Life and Times
   A. Contemporaries
      1. Other famous people alive during your person's lifetime
      2. Presidents and public leaders of the time
   B. Inventions and discoveries
      1. Important inventions of the time period
      2. Discoveries in medicine, science, or exploration
   C. Travel and transportation
      1. How people traveled (boats, horses, other means)
      2. How goods and products were moved
   D. Important events
      1. Wars and conflicts of the time
      2. Disasters (earthquakes, depressions, crashes, etc.)

V. Personal Evaluation
   A. Admirable qualities
   B. Unpleasant behaviors and prejudices
   C. How you feel about your person
   D. Questions you would ask your person if you could
   E. Would you trust this person in your home? (reasons)

Teacher Lesson Plans

Culminating Activity—Western History Day

Set aside one day to be devoted to activities related to your study of the Louisiana Purchase and the Lewis & Clark Expedition. If possible, do this activity with two or three classes at the same grade level. This allows you to share some of the burdens and provides a special experience for the entire grade level.

Costumes

Encourage all of your students to come in costume. Most students could use their famous people costumes. Others would find frontier garb or Native American costumes or clothes with a look of the colonial or early national period. As with the famous people project, ask children to find leather shoes, boots, or moccasins and avoid tennis shoes, which are very modern in concept.

Parent Help

Encourage as many parents or older siblings as you can to come for all or part of the day to enjoy the proceedings and to help set up and monitor the activities. This is truly a day involving the family in the educational process. It helps to survey parents to discover any special talents, interests, or hobbies that would be a match for specific centers.

Centers

- The centers you set up should relate in some way to the expedition or the western frontier or daily life in that time.
- Centers should involve the children in doing an activity and often in making something they can take or put on display.
- The class should be divided into groups of six to seven students.
- Each center should take about 30 minutes, and then students rotate to the next activity.
- The following suggestions will get you started. You will want to add any others for which you have special expertise.

Native American Homes and Villages

This activity could occupy several centers. One center could make Mandan earth lodges and the other tools, weapons, and artifacts of a Mandan village. Another center could focus on the tepees of a Plains Native American tribe such as the Blackfeet or the Crow. A third center could replicate wickiups as used by the Northern Paiute and the Great Basin Native Americans. In all cases, you will need some pictures of these homes and supplies, including craft sticks for interior support, modeling clay, dirt, small pieces of fabric, felt, or construction paper for the tepees, and a supply of small branches.

Building Forts

There were two important forts built by the Lewis & Clark Expedition: Fort Mandan and Fort Clatsop. Students could build either one in a center as a collective project. See *Building Models* (page 42) for details and pictures on this idea.

Teacher Lesson Plans *(cont.)*

Culminating Activity—Western History Day *(cont.)*

Frontier Games

Frontier games included foot races, variations of hide and seek, rolling hoops, flying kites, and snap the whip. A soccer type of kicking game was played in some localities. Toys included tops and marbles. A sports center could feature relay races and one-on-one contests between students in the group. You could also use hula-hoops instead of barrel hoops and have races rolling the hoops with hands. A separate center could feature some of the toys mentioned above.

Map Making

A variety of maps could be created at this center. Use the map section of this book for examples and find others in atlases, encyclopedias, and the Internet. Maps of the Louisiana Territory, the Lewis & Clark Expedition, physical features of the western United States, or Native American locations are among the possibilities. They could be drawn on tag board, large construction paper, or built in three-dimensional form using clay or salt and flour.

Model Pirogue, Raft, or Flatboat

One center could be devoted to model canoes and keelboats as described on *Building Models* (page 42). Be sure to have some tubs available for students to test their constructions.

Eat Hearty

If you have parent volunteers, plan a luncheon with a frontier theme. Parents and students could do the decorations together. Most modern children are far more picky than their frontier counterparts, but you might choose two or three dishes with a frontier flavor. Use *Cooking on the Lewis & Clark Expedition* or *Food and Recipes of the Native Americans* listed in the *Annotated Bibliography* (pages 45–46) for possible recipes.

Literature Selection

If your students have read a literature selection from the time period together, you can set up a center to have them react to the literature selection. Some possible literature selections are described on the *Selected Literature Information* (page 43) sheet.

Other Centers

Other centers could include learning a square dance, performing a Reader's Theater, weaving a simple pattern with yarn, knot-tying, or a simple wood-working project.

Concluding Activity

After your History Day activities or later in the week, show the video with Ken Burns' account of the Lewis & Clark Expedition listed in the *Annotated Bibliography* (pages 45–46).

Name _____

Building Models

Model Pirogue or Dugout Canoe

1. Use two to four ounces of modeling clay to create a model pirogue or dugout canoe. Work the clay to make it soft before you make the model.

2. Try floating your model in a tub of water.

3. See how large a load the model will carry. Use pennies, crayons, craft sticks, or paper clips for weights.

Model Raft or Flatboat

1. Use craft sticks and glue to make a raft. Lay about eight sticks in one direction. Glue three cross sticks to hold the upper sticks in place.

2. Let it dry and then test it in the water to see if it floats.

3. Build a small house to place on the raft to make it a flatboat. Use a craft stick as the rudder. You could try this model with small sticks collected from trees and bushes.

Model Fort Mandan or Fort Clatsop

1. Use craft sticks to create a model of Fort Mandan or Fort Clatsop. Use the pictures shown here as a guide.

2. Use glue and sticks as you did with the boat. Masking tape will also work.

3. Use a firm piece of cardboard or wood as the base. You might want to use modeling clay to help hold the vertical sticks upright.

4. Use crayons or markers to color the wood brown.

Selected Literature Information

Scott O'Dell

Streams to the River, River to the Sea by Scott O'Dell provides a unique insight into Sacagawea's character and experiences. The story begins with Sacagawea's capture by a Minnetarre warrior. She witnesses the burning of her village and sees her mother's scalp hanging from her captor's horse. Reading this book, students can get a sense of the constant fear and danger of being a Native American girl—always at risk from inter-tribal warfare.

The characters in this book are portrayed very realistically with few being all good or all bad. Sacagawea's friendship with Blue Sky, the wife of the Minnetarre chief, makes her life somewhat easier but she still ends up married to the Frenchman, Charbonneau, who wins her in a Native American gambling match.

The arrival of the Lewis & Clark Expedition changes her life even further as she returns to her people, rediscovers friends and relatives among the Shoshone, and provides invaluable assistance to the Corps of Discovery. In the process, she also falls in love.

Boys and girls will enjoy the rapid pace of the book, the many adventures and dangers, the unusual characters, and the unusual perspective of the story told through Native American eyes.

Sing Down the Moon is the story of a Navajo girl who is captured by Spanish soldiers and later escapes only to have her entire village destroyed by American soldiers. Her people move onto a reservation at this point.

Island of the Blue Dolphins chronicles the life of a Native American girl living on the Channel Islands. She ends up stranded on the island by herself. The story of her years alone is filled with courage and adventure.

Gary Paulsen

Students who want a sense of the land that Lewis and Clark traveled through should try *Mr. Tucket* by Gary Paulsen. The story is set in the still unsettled territory explored by Lewis and Clark 40 years before. Francis Tucket is captured by Pawnee Indians and later becomes the traveling partner of a one-armed fur trader and trapper named Jason Grimes. Francis' adventures with the mountain man, Native Americans, and outlaws as he tries to save two children and find his sister are told in the five books of the Tucket series.

Jean Craighead George

Students who want a more modern take on survival in the wild and keeping a wildlife journal should try *My Side of the Mountain* by Jean Craighead George. This story of a boy's decision to live off the land is filled with the how-to's of eating and enjoying your forest neighbors.

Glossary of Terms

ambassador—a representative to another country

astronomy—the study of the stars and planets

botany—the study of plants

cache—a hiding place for supplies

capsize—to overturn in a boat

carcass—dead body

ceded—to give up a piece of land

celestial navigation—using the stars to steer by

concoction—a combination of ingredients

conflict—sharp disagreement, fight, or war

contiguous—next to; touching

corps—a group of people on a mission

desalination—removing salt from sea water

dilemma—a serious problem; a problem with no satisfactory solution

dugout—a wooden boat made by hollowing out a log

eclipse—a darkening of the sun or moon caused by the earth's shadow

expedition—a long journey or voyage

flatboat—a flat-bottomed boat that looks like a raft with a building on it and a pole to steer it

minister—a government representative

hardships—difficult experiences

interpreter—a person who translates from one language to another

keelboat—a wooden boat with curved ends and rounded sides capable of carrying a lot of supplies

marksman—an expert with a weapon

negotiate—to make a deal

pirogue—a large canoe made by hollowing out a log

portable soup—an emergency food supply for the expedition

portage—to carry boats and supplies over land

prejudice—a judgment based on intolerance or hatred

purchase—to buy something; the thing bought

"right of deposit"—the right given to western farmers by the Spanish authorities in Louisiana to export goods from New Orleans without paying a tax

rivermen—frontiersmen who were skilled at moving a keelboat upriver

treaty—an agreement between nations

tributary—a smaller river flowing into a larger one

voyageurs—French fur trappers, traders, and rivermen

1760   1780   1800   1820   1840   1860

Annotated Bibliography

Fiction

George, Jean Craighead. *My Side of the Mountain.* Penguin Putnam, 2001.

Karwoski, Gail Langer. *Seaman: The Dog Who Explored the West with Lewis & Clark.* Peachtree, 1999. (Superb fictionalized account of the expedition from a dog's point of view)

Lasky, Kathryn. *The Journal of Augustus Pelletier.* Scholastic, 2000. (Superior account in journal format of the expedition from the perspective of a fictional member.)

Myers, Laurie. *Lewis & Clark and Me: A Dog's Tale.* St. Martin's, 2002. (Seaman's "first person" account of the trip told with descriptive skill.)

O'Dell, Scott. *Streams to the River, River to the Sea: A Novel of Sacagawea.* Houghton Mifflin, 1986. (Outstanding fictionalized account of Sacagawea's life)

O'Dell, Scott. *Island of the Blue Dolphins.* Bantam, 1971.

O'Dell, Scott. *Sing Down the Moon.* Houghton Mifflin, 1970.

Paulsen, Gary. *Mr. Tucket.* Bantam, 1995. (First of an exciting series of five books set in the 1840s West with all of the dangers faced by Lewis & Clark)

Paulsen, Gary. *Tucket's Ride.* Random House, 1998.

Nonfiction

Ambrose, Stephen E. *Undaunted Courage.* Simon & Schuster, 1997. (Superior historical scholarship expressed in a clear, smooth style)

Barry, James P. *The Louisiana Purchase, April 30, 1803.* Franklin Watts, 1973. (A very lucid account of the negotiations involved in the purchase)

Bergen, Lara. *The Travels of Lewis & Clark.* Steck-Vaughn, 2000. (An easy-to-read account of the journey.)

Biddle, Nicholas (ed.). *The Journals of the Expedition Under the Command of Capts. Lewis & Clark. (2 Volumes).* The Heritage Press, 1962. (This is a reprinting of the classic first publication of the journals in about 1814. Biddle standardized the spelling and usage and streamlined the often repetitious accounts.)

Blumberg, Rhoda. *The Incredible Journey of Lewis & Clark.* Lothrop, Lee & Shepard, 1987. (Very complete intermediate level account of the journey—good maps and black and white illustrations)

Christian, Mary Blount. *Who'd Believe John Colter?* Macmillan, 1993. (A humorous easy-to-read account of the life and adventures of John Colter)

Clark, William. DeVoto, Bernard (ed.). *The Journals of Lewis & Clark.* Houghton Mifflin, 1997. (Contains abridged version of the journals with notes and explanations)

Edwards, Judith. *Lewis & Clark's Journey of Discovery.* Enslow, 1999. (An accurate, well-written account of the voyage with good use of source documents)

Annotated Bibliography *(cont.)*

Nonfiction *(cont.)*

Erdosh, George. *Food and Recipes of the Native Americans.* Rosen Publishing, 1997.

Fitz-Gerald, Christine A. *Meriwether Lewis and William Clark: The Northwest Expedition.* Childrens Press, 1991. (A good, basic intermediate-level text covering the journey—complete and well-illustrated)

Gunderson, Mary. *Cooking on the Lewis & Clark Expedition.* Capstone Press, 2000. (Creates edible, modern-day versions of some foods that were eaten on the expedition)

Hall, Eleanor J. *The Lewis & Clark Expedition.* Lucent, 1996. (Very complete account with excellent sidebars and source documents)

Herbert, Janis. *Lewis & Clark for Kids: Their Journey of Discovery with 21 Activities.* Chicago Review Press, 2000.

Kroll, Steven. *Lewis & Clark: Explorers of the American West.* Holiday House, 1996. (Beautifully illustrated primary book with clear, simple text—a good first book to read to the class)

Myers, Walter Dean. *Toussaint L'Ouverture: The Fight for Haiti's Freedom.* Simon & Schuster, 1996. (Superior primary presentation of L'Ouverture's fight for Haiti's independence—simple text with stark illustrations)

Phelan, Mary Kay. *The Story of the Louisiana Purchase.* Crowell, 1979. (A clear account of the purchase with a good deal of anecdotal detail)

Schmidt, Thomas and Jeremy Schmidt. *The Saga of Lewis and Clark: Into the Uncharted West.* DK Publishing, 2001. (A well-designed, colorful, heavily-illustrated, oversize book with interesting, easy-to-follow text)

Video

Burns, Ken. "Lewis & Clark: The Journey of the Corps of Discovery." Turner Home Entertainment/PBS Video, 1997. (Despite its 240-minute length, the narrative, music, and photography hold the viewers' attention. It would probably be shown in two to four sessions with students.)

Answer Key

The Louisiana Purchase Quiz (page 15)

1. B
2. B
3. C
4. C
5. B
6. C
7. A
8. D
9. B
10. D

The Lewis & Clark Expedition Quiz (page 16)

1. B
2. A
3. C
4. B
5. B
6. D
7. A
8. C
9. B
10. B

The Members of the Corps of Discovery Quiz (page 17)

1. C
2. B
3. C
4. C
5. A
6. C
7. A
8. B
9. C
10. B

The Journey of Lewis & Clark (page 19)

1—The expedition started from here in 1804.

9—The members of the expedition spent the winter of 1805 on the Pacific Coast.

4—The Captains made the decision to follow the south fork of the Missouri River.

3—They built a fort and spent the winter preparing for the journey west.

5—Lewis was threatened by a bear, a mountain lion, and three bull bison in one afternoon.

2—The expedition had a serious and nearly deadly encounter with the Teton Sioux.

8—The Snake and the Columbia Rivers meet here.

6—The Missouri River splits into three branches. The captains named the rivers after important American leaders.

7—They meet the Shoshone and trade for horses.

10—On the way east, the expedition splits in two to explore different routes.

3—Sacagawea and her husband are hired to be guides and interpreters.

11—The expedition reunites for the return trip down the Missouri River.

5—There are five waterfalls here on the Missouri River that the expedition had to walk around.

1—The expedition ended here on September 23, 1806.

Answer Key (cont.)

The Louisiana Purchase (page 20)

Montana	1889
North Dakota	1889
South Dakota	1889
Wyoming	1890
Nebraska	1867
Colorado	1876
Kansas	1861
New Mexico	1912
Oklahoma	1907
Louisiana	1812
Arkansas	1836
Missouri	1821
Iowa	1846
Minnesota	1858
Texas	1845

3. The 13 original states are: Delaware, Pennsylvania, New Jersey, Georgia, Connecticut, Massachusetts, Maryland, South Carolina, New Hampshire, Virginia, New York, North Carolina, and Rhode Island.

4. The four new states admitted to the union before the Louisiana Purchase are: Vermont, Kentucky, Tennessee, and Ohio.

The Growth of the United States (page 21)

1. Louisiana Purchase Territory
2. 13 original states
3. Mississippi River
4. Red River Basin
5. Florida
6. Texas, Mexican Cession, Oregon Country
7. Gadsden Purchase
8. Texas
9. 1867
10. 1898
11. Louisiana Purchase and Oregon Country
12. Alaska and Hawaii

Native Americans on the Map (page 22)

1. Plains Native Americans: Sioux, Crow, Cheyenne, Hidatsa, Mandan, Kiowa, Blackfeet, Arapaho, Osage, Oto, and Kansa
2. California-Intermountain Native Americans: Shoshone, Bannock, Ute, Paiute, Nez Perce, Flathead, and Yakima
3. Pacific Coast tribes: Chinook, Yaquina, and Siuslaw
4. Plains
5. California-Intermountain
6. California-Intermountain
7. Plains
8. Plains
9. North Dakota
10. Idaho
11. Oklahoma
12. Washington
13. Montana
14. No
15. Nez Perce and Blackfeet
16. Kansas